Folk Latin America

The Fool, The Trickster, The Hero

By Vivian M. Cuesta
Illustrated by Ande Cook

CELEBRATION PRESS
Pearson Learning Group

Contents

The Silly Armadillo

In the beautiful country of Peru, there once lived an armadillo. He was a silly armadillo and liked to decorate his hut with all sorts of curious-looking things. Strings of berries hung from the windows, and bird nests perched atop the doorways.

The little armadillo thought his decorations were very clever and creative. He was especially proud of his weaving. He wove amazing designs on his loom. Then he made them into hats. His friends, Llama and Fox, thought his hats were a little silly, but they always told Armadillo they liked them anyway.

One day as Armadillo was sticking marigolds into a new purple hat he'd made, he heard Llama and Fox coming up the road.

"Hello, my friends," Armadillo called out. "How are you this lovely day?"

Llama and Fox grinned at Armadillo.

"Guess what!" cried Llama.

"What?" said Armadillo.

"I have wonderful news!" Llama went on. "King Lion is going to have a fiesta at the lake. All the animals of Peru are invited!"

"It's his birthday, so it will be a big party!" added Fox excitedly.

"A big fiesta?" cried Armadillo.

"Yes!" Llama and Fox answered together.

"All the animals of Peru are invited?" asked Armadillo.

"Yes!" Llama and Fox said again.

"And the king himself has invited us?" cried Armadillo.

"YES!" Llama and Fox shouted.

Armadillo frowned as a huge cloud of worry surrounded him.

"Oh, dear. Oh, dear! Whatever will I wear?" cried the silly armadillo.

"Oh, don't be so silly," scolded Llama. "No one will care what you are wearing."

"Don't be so silly," added Fox. "Animals aren't supposed to wear fancy clothes."

Armadillo *was* silly, though. He was so silly that he didn't even know he was silly. He thought that if he wore fancy clothes everyone would think he was important.

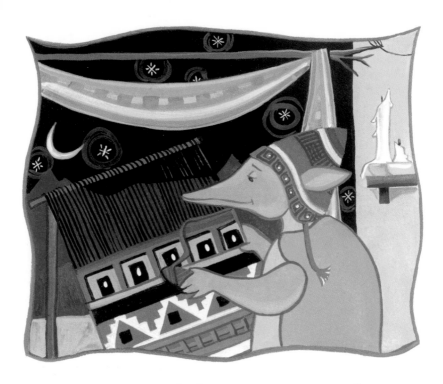

Armadillo decided to weave a coat of many colors for the fiesta. Then he would be the best dressed armadillo anyone had ever seen. He worked day and night, weaving the brightest colors of glowing orange, peacock blue, fire red, sparkling gold, fern green, shining silver, and royal purple into his fancy coat.

Armadillo's coat was almost ready, and he could hardly wait for the day of the party. He was sure that when everyone there saw his coat, they would wish to have one just like it.

Just then, Llama poked his head through the window of Armadillo's hut. "Are you ready to make your grand entrance at the party tonight?" he asked.

"What?" cried Armadillo. "Tonight? The fiesta can't be tonight! I thought it was next week!"

"Well," said Llama, "you must have gotten your days mixed up. How can you remember anything when all you think about is your silly coat?"

"Oh, dear. My coat! It's not finished! What will I do?" cried Armadillo. He started weaving as fast as he could. He had to finish his coat before the party or all his grand dreams would be ruined.

Armadillo finished his coat just in time for the party. The top half was neat and beautiful, but the bottom half was messy and ugly. He had hurried too much to finish it.

Armadillo couldn't see that, though. He proudly walked into the party still dreaming that his coat would amaze everyone.

"How silly," the animals all whispered when they saw him. "What a silly coat! What a silly armadillo! Ha! Ha! Ha!"

Armadillo was so ashamed that he ran away from the party. He had been so sure that all the other animals would admire his coat and be jealous of his grand appearance. Now he knew the truth.

Armadillo knew he had made himself a laughingstock with his silly vanity and pride. He decided to wear his silly coat forever to remind himself of his foolish mistake. The Incans say this is why the armadillo lives in a burrow under the earth and hardly ever comes out except at night: He is ashamed for being so silly over his foolish coat.

The Rabbit in the Moon

Some people say that there is a man in the moon. Some people say that the moon is made of cheese. Coyote knows that there is a rabbit in the moon. He also knows how this very clever rabbit got to the moon in the first place.

Once there was an old man and woman who owned a rabbit and a coyote. They were very poor, though. One day they were so hungry that they decided to eat the rabbit. They had no choice.

The old woman sadly locked the rabbit in its cage made of twigs and began to boil some water. Coyote saw this and smiled.

Coyote didn't like Rabbit. Rabbit was just too clever. Rabbit always seemed to fool Coyote. Coyote didn't like that at all.

Now he went over to Rabbit's cage and said, "Rabbit, it looks like you are going to be tonight's supper. The old people are going to cook you and eat you, and they will give me some, too." Coyote grinned.

Rabbit really was too clever for Coyote. Now his ears twitched, his nose wiggled, and his eyes twinkled. He had an idea.

"Oh, Coyote," he said, "you are so silly. They are not going to cook me. They are boiling water to make hot chocolate."

"That's not true!" cried Coyote. "They are going to eat you!"

"Oh, no," said Rabbit. "The old woman told me to wait in my cage and she would give me the first helping of chocolate. If you want, you can wait in here, and she will give you the first helping instead."

Coyote was so excited at the idea of getting chocolate before Rabbit did that he unlocked the cage and got in. Rabbit quickly ran off as Coyote waited patiently inside the cage. After an hour or so, Coyote began to realize he had been tricked. Rabbit had fooled him again!

Now Coyote was so angry that he broke the cage and ran off after Rabbit. Coyote was not very smart, but he was a very fast runner. Soon he caught up with Rabbit in the forest hiding among some rocks. "You tricked me for the last time, Rabbit!" shouted Coyote. "This time you won't get away with it! I want that chocolate!"

Rabbit's ears twitched, his nose wiggled, and his eyes twinkled. He had an idea.

"Why, excuse me," said Rabbit, looking surprised. "I'm sorry, but I don't know what you are talking about. You must have confused me with someone else."

"Do you mean you're not the rabbit who tricked me?" Coyote asked.

"Nope," said Rabbit. "I'm sorry I don't have any chocolate for you, but I have an even bigger problem. I need a place to hide in a hurry because the sky is falling."

"Oh, no!" said Coyote. "Maybe I should hide, too."

"Help me lift this big rock," said Rabbit. "We can both hide under it. You hold it while I find a stick to prop it up."

So Coyote, who was now very worried about the sky falling, lifted the big, flat rock and held it up while the rabbit hopped off.

Coyote waited and waited for the rabbit to come back. He began to grow tired from holding up the big rock. Finally he realized it was the same rabbit all along. He had been tricked again.

Now Coyote was really mad. First Rabbit had tricked Coyote into helping him escape so he wouldn't be eaten. Then Rabbit had pretended to be someone else and made Coyote think the sky was falling so he could escape again! Coyote let go of the rock. He ran off to find Rabbit, angrier than ever.

This time Coyote found Rabbit swinging on a vine high over the lake and laughing loudly at how he had tricked Coyote. Coyote yanked on the vine, and Rabbit flew up into the night sky. As Rabbit flew past the moon, the moon goddess reached out and grabbed him in her arms. She loved rabbits, especially clever ones.

As the moon goddess held him, Rabbit's ears twitched, his nose wiggled, and his eyes twinkled. He had escaped again.

To this day, when the moon is full, you can still see the outline of the rabbit, safe with the moon goddess. As for Coyote, he howls at the moon each night, still angry at the clever little rabbit that tricked him.

The Lucky Charm

Deep in the jungle of Guatemala, there is a Mayan treasure. You won't find this treasure buried in the ground. You won't find it under a rock. You can only see this treasure high in a tree or flying through the sky. This Mayan treasure is the quetzal, a magical bird. It has dark green wings, a bright red chest, and a long blue tail.

If you listen carefully when the wind blows through the jungle, you might hear the quetzal. Sometimes it will perch in a tree to whisper the secret of how it was born.

A long time ago in a Mayan village, there lived an old man who told fortunes. Everyone believed he had magical powers and knew what was going to happen in the future.

One day the entire village gathered for a huge party. The chief and his wife were celebrating the birth of their baby son, Quetzal. The fortune teller gave the baby a special blessing. He said Quetzal would grow up to be wise and good. This made the people very happy.

The old man knew that the future had even more in store for Quetzal. He did not want to reveal this secret, however, until the time was right.

Not everyone was happy about the chief's new son. The chief's brother, Chiruma, knew that when the chief died, Quetzal would become chief. This made Chiruma very jealous. He wanted to be chief instead.

As Quetzal grew up, he became all of the things that the old man had said. Everyone in the village loved him very much.

Quetzal was a great hunter and fisherman. He showed strength and courage in everything he did. Quetzal learned from his father all about the duties of a chief. He learned that a good leader should be wise, fair, and brave. Quetzal's father knew that Quetzal would be a great chief someday.

One morning, Quetzal went to his father's hut to wake him for a tribal meeting. The good chief did not wake up, though. He had died peacefully in his sleep. Quetzal and the people were very sad.

All of the villagers gathered for their beloved chief's funeral. Then the villagers bowed to Quetzal. Now he was chief.

The fortune teller knew it was time to reveal his secret. He placed a necklace with a blue feather charm around Quetzal's neck. He said, "Quetzal will be a great chief. This charm will protect him. The gods say he is very special and will live forever."

Quetzal became a wise and trusted leader. One day the village was attacked. Quetzal and the other warriors rushed into battle. The warriors were amazed when all of the arrows aimed at Quetzal simply stopped in mid-air and fell to the ground. The other tribe ran away in fear. Quetzal's lucky charm had kept him safe.

Quetzal's success made Chiruma even more jealous. He wanted to get rid of Quetzal for good. One night Chiruma sneaked quietly into Quetzal's hut and stole the lucky charm while Quetzal was sleeping. When Quetzal awoke, he saw that the charm was gone. In a panic he ran to the fortune teller's hut.

Chiruma was prepared for this and was
hiding behind the hut. When Quetzal came
near, he shot an arrow straight at Quetzal's
heart. Without his lucky charm, the arrow
hit Quetzal, and he was killed. The old
man, hearing Quetzal's cries, rushed out
of the hut. He saw Quetzal dead on the
ground and Chiruma running away.

The old man knew that the lucky charm would only protect Quetzal, not Chiruma. He would make sure that Chiruma was punished. As for Quetzal, the gods kept their promise. His body was changed into a beautiful bird with a long, shimmering blue tail. The Mayan people honor the quetzal to remember the brave, young chief who will live forever.